WHAT IS PASSOVER?

WRITTEN BY
SHARI LAST

FESTIVAL OF FREEDOM

What do you know about Passover?

This Jewish festival has a lot of rules. Rules about what to eat and what not to eat. Rules about a big meal called the Seder. Many of the rules might seem funny or strange to you. But, like most other Jewish festivals, Passover is about spending time with family, remembering an important part of the history of the Jewish people, and eating lots of traditional foods!

LET'S FIND OUT MORE ABOUT PASSOVER!

PASS OVER WHAT?

The festival got its name from the part of the story where God "passed over" the Jewish houses while bringing punishments down on the houses of their enemies. What punishments? Why? Read on to find out!

WHEN IS PASSOVER?

Passover is an eight-day festival. It starts on the 15th of the Jewish month of Nissan.

The Jewish calendar is lunar (it follows the cycles of the moon, not the sun) so its dates don't line up with "regular" dates each year. Passover can fall any time between late March and late April.

DID YOU KNOW? Passover often falls close to – or even on the same day as – the Christian holiday Easter. However, the two holidays are not based on the same stories or events.

In Israel, Passover lasts for seven days, which is actually how long it's supposed to be. In the olden days, Jewish people who lived outside Israel were never quite sure when the festivals were supposed to begin, so they added on an extra day just to be sure!

PASSOVER OR PESACH?

In Hebrew, the name of this festival is Pesach. This is pronounced *peh-such*.

Note: the "ch" in "Sameach" is a sound you make at the back of your throat. Or you can pronounce it like this: *peh-sukh*.

Pesach means "pass over", so that's easy enough to remember!

Here's how it's written in Hebrew:

פסח

THE STORY OF PASSOVER

Are you ready to journey back in time to ancient Egypt? Let's go . . .

For 210 years, the Jewish people (sometimes known as the Hebrews) had been slaves to King Pharaoh, Ramses II. Pharaoh forced the Jewish slaves to build his magnificent cities, temples, and pyramids. He even demanded they make their own bricks in the hot, hot sun. He piled on more and more work every day.

Moses was a Jew who grew up in Pharaoh's palace, though he didn't realise he was Jewish until he was older. Once he found out, he ran away. When he was 80 years old, Moses returned. God had commanded him to lead his people out of Egypt.

Moses asked Pharaoh to let the Jewish people go, but Pharaoh said, "No." This is when God punished the Egyptian people with the Ten Plagues — ten terrible plagues that were meant to convince Pharaoh to let the slaves go.

THE TEN PLAGUES

The Ten Plagues were awful for the Egyptians but, miraculously, the Jewish people not affected by the plagues. If only Pharaoh had just let the slaves go!

1. **Blood**
   All the water in Egypt turned to blood. The Egyptians had nothing to drink!
2. **Frogs**
   A plague of frogs swept across the country.
3. **Lice**
   An outbreak of lice made the Egyptians very itchy.
4. **Wild Animals**
   Terrifying beasts wandered across the land.
5. **Pestilence**
   The Egyptians' farm animals got sick and died.
6. **Boils**
   The Egyptians were covered in painful boils.
7. **Hailstones**
   Huge hailstones crashed down on Egypt. Some say they had fire inside!
8. **Locusts**
   Swarms of locusts devoured Egypt's plants and trees
9. **Darkness**
   Six days of pitch-black darkness made life unbearable.
10. **Death of the Firstborns**
    The eldest son in every Egyptian household would die.

Pharaoh was able to avoid the worst of the early plagues, thanks to his wealth and power. He refused to let the slaves go. But the plagues continued and the Egyptians grew scared. Then, when Pharaoh heard about the final plague, he panicked. Pharaoh himself was a firstborn!

The terrible tenth plague was coming, and God told Moses how to protect the Jewish people. The angel of death would pass over any house that had the blood of a lamb on its doorposts. So the Jewish people sacrificed lambs and painted the blood on their houses.

That night, as death swept through Egypt, Pharaoh ran through the night to find Moses. "Go immediately!" he said. "Go!"

Moses spread the word among the Jewish people: they must pack up and leave right away — before Pharaoh changed his mind. The Jewish people gathered their belongings and prepared food for the long journey ahead. They didn't have time to wait for their bread to rise, so they just baked it and left.

About a week after they left Egypt, the Jewish people came to the Red Sea. With horror, they realised that Pharaoh and his army were chasing them, trying to get their slaves back. They were trapped . . . until God performed another miracle. He split the sea! The Jewish people walked between the water on a path of dry land. When Pharaoh and his soldiers chased after them, the waters collapsed, destroying the Egyptian army.

They ate the lamb as part of their last meal in Egypt, along with bitter herbs and matzah. (Matzah is bread that hasn't risen like the soft, yummy bread you eat! Matzah is flat and hard, like burnt pita, or crackers. This is the sort of "bread" the slaves got to eat.)

And that was it — the Jewish slaves walked out of Egypt, free at last.

Eight Days of Passover

On Passover, Jewish people remember the miracles God performed that led to freedom for the slaves.

Here are some of the things we do on Passover to remember:

- We sit around the dinner table and discuss the whole Passover story, asking questions and trying to learn as much as we can about it. This is called the Seder.

- We do things that remind us how horrible slavery was, such as eating matzah and bitter herbs.

- We do things that remind us how wonderful it is to be free, such as drinking wine and singing songs.

- We eat matzah over the whole of Passover as a symbol of the slaves' journey from slavery to freedom.

DAY BY DAY

Passover lasts for eight days. The first two days are "festival" days, so they are like Shabbat — when Jewish people cannot drive, cook, write, work, go to school, spend money, or use electronic devices.

Then there are four days when we *can* do all those things, but we still can't eat regular bread. These four days are called "chol hamoed". The last two days are "festival" days again.

In Israel, there is one festival day, five days of chol hamoed, and then one final festival day.

FAMILY FUN

It is traditional that even on the days of chol hamoed, Jewish people don't work or go to school, so these days are normally filled with family outings and hikes, which are often known as "matzah rambles"!

Hey, where's the matzah?

HAVE YOU HEARD ABOUT CHAMETZ?

Chametz is food that is forbidden on Passover. It includes all bread that has risen (which is pretty much any bread, bagel, pita, roll, bun, or baguette, etc). In fact, the only "bread" you can eat on Passover is matzah — a flat, crunchy cracker that reminds us of the bread the slaves ate in Egypt, as well as the bread they baked quickly (so it didn't have time to rise) once they were freed.

Chametz also includes any food that contains flour, and which has been baked for more than 18 minutes. So this includes all breads, and also biscuits and cakes, too. But don't worry! There are plenty of Passover cake and cookie recipes! We just follow what I guess is a gluten-free diet (apart from all the matzah, of course).

PASSOVER PREP

The rules about chametz are very strict. We cannot have even a crumb of chametz in the house! So before Passover, you might notice your Jewish friends doing a lot of cleaning. A LOT. Every inch of our house must be chametz free.

We clean the kitchen like it's never been cleaned before, plus we go through each room — bookshelves, wardrobes, under the bed — and the car. Once, my friend's dad washed all the LEGO in the dishwasher because it was covered in crumbs!

My parents usually give me a list of where to look for chametz among my stuff:

- Bedside table drawers
- The pockets of all my clothes (I always find some chametz there!)
- Toy boxes
- School bag

We can't use our regular kitchen stuff on Passover because it's touched chametz. We have a special Passover cupboard, with Passover pots, pans, cutlery, plates, serving spoons, cups — you get the picture! We cover our kitchen counters too, as they have also touched chametz. It's a lot of work, but . . . actually, that's it. It's just a lot of work.

SEDER NIGHT

Ooh, I love Seder night!

Seder night is the first night of Passover, when we get to stay up really late and have a huge, long meal with lots of fun things to do and sing plenty of songs! The Seder is full of references to the Passover story and we carry out actions and eat foods that symbolise how the Jewish people went from being slaves to being free.

SEDER PLATE

This is the most important thing to go on the Seder table. You fill it with items of food that symbolise different parts of the Passover story. You will eat most of them during the Seder.

You can use any plate, although many families have special Seder plates like this one, that tell you where to put everything.

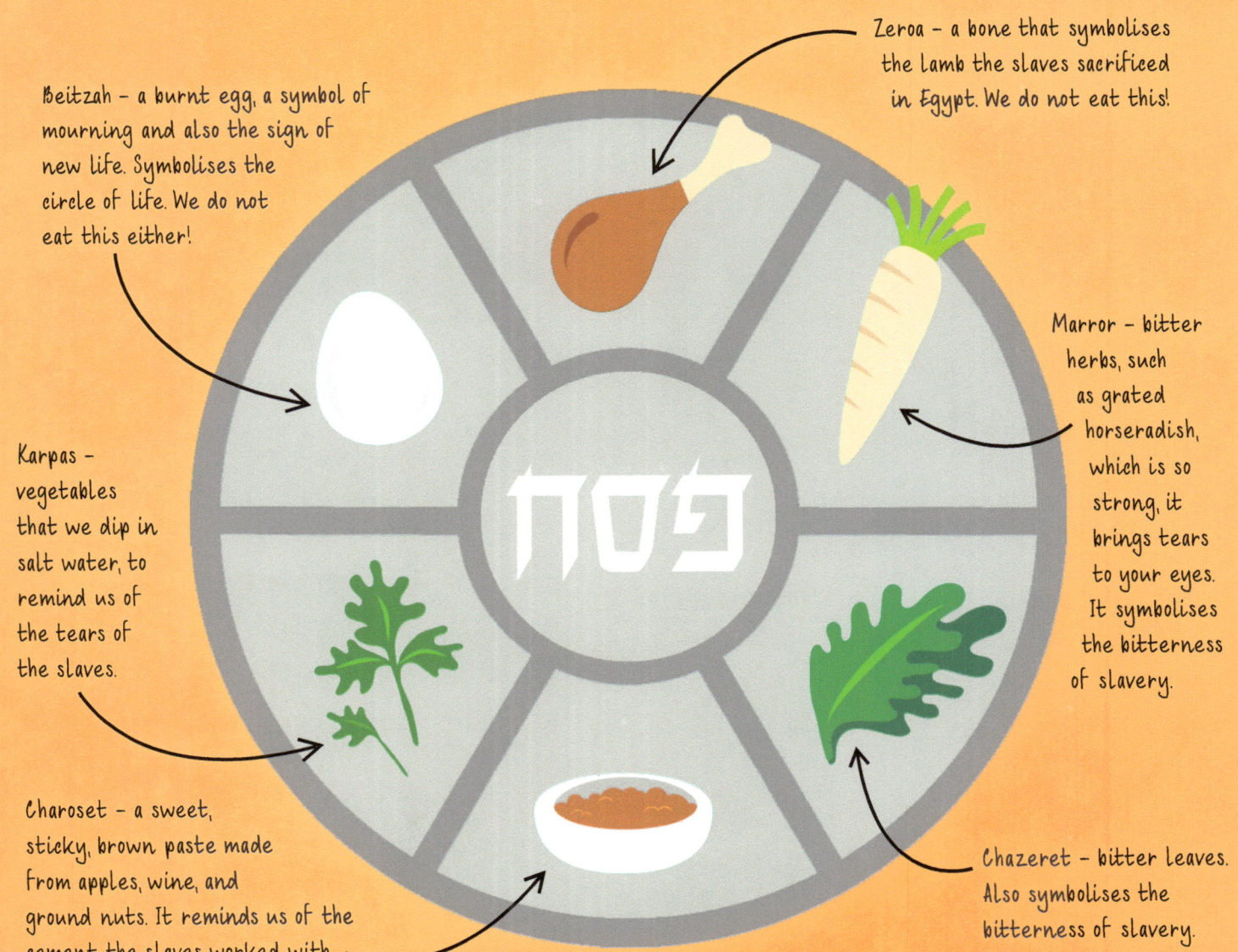

Zeroa – a bone that symbolises the lamb the slaves sacrificed in Egypt. We do not eat this!

Beitzah – a burnt egg, a symbol of mourning and also the sign of new life. Symbolises the circle of life. We do not eat this either!

Marror – bitter herbs, such as grated horseradish, which is so strong, it brings tears to your eyes. It symbolises the bitterness of slavery.

Karpas – vegetables that we dip in salt water, to remind us of the tears of the slaves.

Charoset – a sweet, sticky, brown paste made from apples, wine, and ground nuts. It reminds us of the cement the slaves worked with.

Chazeret – bitter leaves. Also symbolises the bitterness of slavery.

Kadesh

Urchatz

Karpas

ORDER OF THE SEDER

Seder means "order" in Hebrew, because there is a whole order of things to do as part of the Seder. Here's the full list:

Kadesh Say a blessing on the first cup of wine

Urchatz Wash hands – no blessing

Karpas Dip vegetables in salt water

Yachatz Break the middle matzah in two and hide the bigger half. This is the afikoman

Maggid Tell the story of Passover and discuss it as much as you can

Rachtzah Wash hands, this time with a blessing

Motzi Matzah Say a blessing over the matzah and eat some

Maror Eat bitter herbs

Korech Eat a sandwich of matzah and bitter herbs

Shulchan Orech Eat dinner!

Zafun Eat the afikoman

Barech Say a blessing after the meal

Hallel Prayers of praise

Nirtzah Final songs

HAGGADAH
This is the book we use during the Seder. It has all the blessings, songs, and words for each part.

FOUR CUPS OF WINE

During the Seder, we drink four cups of wine. Yes, four. Don't worry, you can drink grape juice instead. But trust me, four cups — even of grape juice — is a lot! We drink four cups to celebrate each of the four words God used to promise the slaves their freedom. One cup per word.

DID YOU KNOW?

You can buy all sorts of Haggadahs. Mine is a children's Haggadah and it has really funny pictures. My dad's Haggadah has instructions, such as: *Pour the second cup of wine now* and *Point to the bitter herbs while you say the next paragraph.* My sister has a Harry Potter Haggadah! She loves it.

THREE MATZAHS

Three matzahs are used during the Seder. We use different matzahs for different parts of the Seder.

MAH NISHTANAH (THE FOUR QUESTIONS)

There is a part of the Seder (during Maggid) when the youngest child asks four questions about why Seder night is different to all other nights. This is usually my job as the youngest, though I get a bit shy if we have a lot of guests! (Luckily, everyone joins in with me if I ask them to!)

Seder night is all about discussing and analysing the story of Passover, so asking questions is encouraged — especially of young children. That's why we say the Mah Nishtanah.

ELIJAH'S CUP

A special cup is set out on the Seder table and, after the meal, it is filled with wine for Elijah the Prophet, who is said to visit every Seder. Someone goes to open the front door for Elijah, while all the kids take this opportunity to watch the wine in the cup to see if our invisible guest drinks any!

AFIKOMAN

Near the beginning of the Seder, we break the middle matzah and hide part of it. That part is called the afikoman. Here's where it gets fun: as we near the end, it is time to eat the afikoman. The Seder cannot continue without it.

But... the kids at the table were watching to see where the afikoman was hidden earlier. They will have found it by now and hidden it themselves. And they won't return it until the adults have agreed to a gift in exchange!

SECOND SEDER

Some people who keep eight days of Passover will have a second Seder on the second night of Passover. It is exactly the same as the first night (except everyone is a lot less excited about it).

TRADITIONAL FOODS

MATZAH

There are lots of rules about food on Passover, so the most obvious Passover food is matzah — the closest you can get to a slice of bread during this holiday. Breakfast will often be matzah with cheese, matzah with jam — or my favourite — matzah with butter.

Matzah Brei
A breakfast treat for me is matzah brei. It's like matzah French toast. We fry pieces of matzah in egg. Sprinkle some sugar or drizzle honey on top and it's delicious!

EGGS

Eggs are often eaten on Passover: scrambled, fried, and hard-boiled. Hard-boiled eggs and matzah are a typical packed lunch for families to take on their matzah rambles.

Egg in Salt Water
At Seder night, a traditional starter is a hard-boiled egg in salt water. It's actually quite yummy!

POTATOES

Another Passover staple is the potato. Baked potato, mashed potatoes, roast potatoes, and chips. It's hard to live without the potato on Passover!

Kugel

Potato kugel is eaten all year round, but often makes an appearance at Passover. It is a dish of grated potatoes, onions, and eggs, sort of like a dairy-free potato quiche.

MARROR

The bitter herbs eaten on Seder night are most often grated raw horseradish. Depending on how strong the horseradish is and how recently you grated it, marror can be really strong! Once, it actually made my dad cry. It was hilarious!

CHAROSET

This sticky apple, wine, and nut paste is used at the Seder, but my family likes it so much, we eat it on matzah over the whole of Passover.

AROUND THE WORLD

Passover is all about remembering how the Jewish people went from being slaves to being free. Different cultures have their own unique ways of remembering — from acting out parts of it the story to the foods they eat.

SPAIN
The leader of the Seder carries the Seder plate round the table three times, tapping it on each guest's head as a blessing.

ROMANIA
To understand how hard the slavery was, Romanian Jews fill a pillowcase with heavy objects and take turns carrying it around the Seder table.

NEPAL
Every year, "The Seder on Top of the World" takes place in Kathmandu, near Mount Everest. Thousands of Jewish backpackers gather here for a huge Passover Seder.

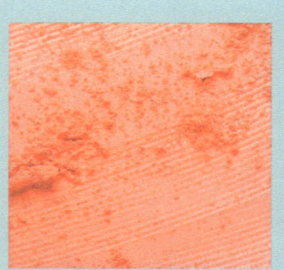

GIBRALTAR
It is traditional to add a little bit of brick dust to the charoset, so it is really like cement!

ORANGES
Around the world, some families add an orange to their Seder plate to symbolise the inclusion of the LGBTQ+ community.

ETHIOPIA
Families enjoy homemade matzah, often made with chickpea flour. Many break their old dishes and cooking utensils and buy or make new ones for Passover.

INDIA
Indian Jews add a Pharaoh's Cup to their Seder table. They fill it with wine and then pour it out into everyone's glasses, symbolising how Pharaoh's stubbornness was taken away.

IRAN
Many Iranian Jews playfully whip each other with spring onions (scallions) during the Seder. This symbolises the harsh treatment of the slaves in Egypt.

SYRIA
Syrian Jews act out leaving Egypt in a hurry: they throw pieces of matzah into a backpack and wear it on their shoulders.

MIRIAM'S CUP
Some add Miriam's Cup next to Elijah's and fill it with water in honour of Miriam, Moses's sister.

HUNGARY
Placing jewellery on the Seder table symbolises the gold and silver given by the Egyptians to make the slaves leave quickly.

PASSOVER GREETINGS

I hope you've enjoyed learning about Passover. If you have any Jewish friends and you want to wish them a happy Passover, here are a few ways to say it:

"HAPPY PASSOVER!"

"PESACH SAMEACH!"

Pronunciation: *Peh-such Sum-ay-uch*
(This means "Happy Pesach" in Hebrew)

CHAG PESACH KASHER V'SAMEACH

Pronunciation: *Chuhg Peh-such Kuh-sher Veh-sum-ay-uch*
(This mean "A happy and kosher Pesach" in Hebrew)

And since Passover marks the start of the summer season, a traditional greeting in the days right after Passover is the Yiddish greeting:

"A GITTIN ZIMMER!"

Pronunciation: *Ah Git-in Zim-er*
(This mean "Good summer!" in Yiddish)

> **NOTE**
> The "ch" in "Chag", "Pesach", and "Sameach" is a guttural sound you make at the back of your throat. Or you can just use an "h" sound.

LET'S MAKE CHAROSET!

Charoset is meant to look like the cement the slaves used in Egypt, even though it tastes quite nice! Different Jewish cultures have different charoset recipes. Here is my family recipe.

Ingredients
- 3 apples, grated
- 3 tablespoons ground almonds
- 2 tablespoons ground walnuts
- 2 tablespoons wine
- 1 tablespoons sugar
- 1 tsp cinnamon

Method
Mix all the ingredients together. The beauty of charoset is that you can adjust the flavour to your taste. Add less sugar if you don't want it too sweet. Add more nuts if you like a thicker consistency.

Ingredients
- 1 box matzah
- water
- frosting or chocolate spread
- sprinkles

LET'S MAKE MATZAH CAKE!

Method

Dip a piece of matzah into water for 30 seconds, then place onto a tray. Spread frosting or chocolate spread on it and then repeat. Top the final piece of matzah with extra frosting/spread and then add sprinkles. Cover tightly and refrigerate overnight.

TAKE THE QUIZ

Let's test your Passover knowledge!
(Answers at the bottom of the page.)

1. How many days does Passover last?
2. How many days does it last in Israel?
3. Who led the Jews out of Egypt?
4. How many plagues were there?
5. Why is Passover called Passover?
6. How many cups of wine are drunk at Seder?
7. How many matzahs are used at Seder?
8. Name three things that go on the Seder plate?
9. Who sings the Mah Nishtanah?
10. Which historical figure is said to visit every Seder on Passover?
11. What is the afikoman?
12. Why do some people hit each other with spring onions at their Seder?

Quiz Answers: 1. Eight 2. Seven 3. Moses 4. Ten 5. The angel of death passed over the Jewish houses and didn't kill their firstborns 6. Four 7. Three 8. Zeroa (bone), Beitzah (burnt egg), Marror (bitter herbs), Chazeret (bitter leaves), Charoset (sweet paste), Karpas (vegetables) 9. The youngest child 10. Elijah the Prophet 11. A piece of the middle matzah that is hidden and eaten at the end of the Seder. 12. To remember how the slaves were treated

PASSOVER CRAFT IDEAS

DECORATE THE SEDER TABLE

Turn your Seder table into an amazing Passover scene. Build cardboard pyramids, add your own trees or LEGO people to form a crowd of slaves walking out of Egypt. You could even arrange blue and sand-coloured tablecloths to make a "splitting-of-the-sea" scene!

DESIGN YOUR OWN AFIKOMAN BAG

It's nice to have an afikoman bag to keep this precious — but crumbly — piece of matzah safe. Fold a piece of paper and tape the edges down to create an envelope, or you could staple the edges of fabric together to form a bag. Decorate with markers or stickers!

DECORATE A CUP FOR ELIJAH

Find an old glass or cup (check with a parent first!) or a disposable cup and decorate it for the important but invisible guest, Elijah the Prophet. My brother once decorated a cup so beautifully, it has sort of become a family heirloom — we use it every year!

MAKE YOUR OWN TEN PLAGUES

My family gives little "Plague Packs" to each child for Seder night. Each contains something that refers to each of the plagues. (A small cup of red jelly for blood, toy frogs, chocolate sprinkles for lice, toy animals, cotton balls for hailstones — which we all enjoy throwing at one another — and sunglasses for darkness.) What else can you think of?

First published in Great Britain in 2024
by **TELL ME MORE Books**

Text copyright ©2024 Shari Last
Design copyright ©2024 Shari Last

ISBN: 978-1-917200-00-4

Picture credits: Thanks to Adobe Stock; Elia Pellegrini and Mathew Macquarrie at Unsplash; and Rafael Ben-Ari, Hadasit, Dionisvera, Elzbieta Sekowska, Roman Yanushevsky, Maglara, Cabeca de Marmore, Moti Meiri, and Studio Evasion at Shutterstock.com.

All rights reserved. Without limiting the rights under the copyright reserved above, no part of this publication may be reproduced, stored in, or introduced into a retrieval system, or transmitted, in any form, or by any means (electronic, mechanical, photocopying, recording or otherwise), without the prior written permission of the copyright owner.

WWW.TELLMEMOREBOOKS.COM

www.ingramcontent.com/pod-product-compliance
Lightning Source LLC
Chambersburg PA
CBHW050748110526
44591CB00002B/18